TULSA CITY-COUNTY LIBRARY

hRjc

D1237636

TULSA CITY-COUNTY LIBRARY

Gun Education and Safety

GUNS & SPECIAL WEAPONS

BRIAN KEVIN

ABDO Publishing Company

visit us at
www.abdopublishing.com

Published by ABDO Publishing Company, PO Box 398166, Minneapolis, MN 55439.
Copyright © 2012 by Abdo Consulting Group, Inc. International copyrights reserved in all
countries. No part of this book may be reproduced in any form without written permission from the
publisher. The Checkerboard Library™ is a trademark and logo of ABDO Publishing Company.

Printed in the United States of America, North Mankato, Minnesota.
112011
012012

 PRINTED ON RECYCLED PAPER

Cover Photo: U.S. Navy
Interior Photos: Alamy p. 6; AP Images pp. 25, 29; Corbis pp. 7, 27; Getty Images pp. 19, 20–21,
    21, 25, 28; Glow Images pp. 7, 9, 23; iStockphoto pp. 8, 26; Photo Researchers pp. 4–5;
    Photo Courtesy of U.S. Army pp. 10, 11, 12, 16, 18; U.S. Marine Corps pp. 14–15, 17

Series Coordinator: Megan M. Gunderson
Editors: Megan M. Gunderson, BreAnn Rumsch
Art Direction: Neil Klinepier

Library of Congress Cataloging-in-Publication Data

Kevin, Brian, 1980-
  Guns & special weapons / Brian Kevin.
    p. cm. -- (Gun education and safety)
  Includes index.
  ISBN 978-1-61783-319-9
  1. Firearms--Juvenile literature. 2. Weapons--Juvenile literature. I. Title. II. Title: Guns and
special weapons.
  TS534.5.K47 2012
  683.4--dc23
                        2011031612

CONTENTS

Gabriela had been around guns since she was a young girl. She had passed hunter's safety class when she was 10. When she was 12, she had shot her first turkey. Some weekends, her dad took her to the shooting range. Gabriela thought she knew a thing or two about guns. Boy, was she wrong!

One day, Gabriela's class took a field trip to the local police department. Officer Bradley served as its

An armory allows police officers to become familiar with a variety of weapons.

guide. He asked Gabriela and her classmates if they wanted to see the armory. This was where the police stored their weapons and other equipment. Officer Bradley led the eager class inside.

Gabriela had never seen anything like these weapons! Officer Bradley even let her handle a deactivated Taser. It was far different from a hunting rifle or a handgun. Police could use it to stop criminals without injuring them.

Officer Bradley said there are many special kinds of guns. Some kinds, he said, only the police should use. That made sense to Gabriela. She couldn't imagine hunting turkeys with a Taser!

Combination Guns

As early as the 1500s, gun makers were creating special weapons. During this time, guns were unreliable. Sometimes, they didn't fire when they were supposed to. And many were difficult to aim successfully.

So, some gunsmiths combined guns with other weapons. The additional weapon was like giving the shooter a back-up plan.

In England, King Henry VIII's men used shields that had guns in the middle. The gun was a **breech**-loading matchlock pistol. Its short barrel stuck out of the shield's face.

Behind the shield were the matchlock **mechanism** and the **trigger**. So, a gunman could fire the weapon while shielded from danger.

On a matchlock weapon, there was a lit match. Pulling the trigger touched the match to gunpowder, which caused the weapon to fire.

Modern law enforcement officers still use shields and guns. But today, these are separate tools.

Many gun-shields were made in Italy in the 1500s.

Guns with swords or knives attached to them were popular from the 1600s to the 1900s. These sharp gun attachments are called bayonets.

In the 1600s, European gun makers combined guns with axes. There were many different versions of this weapon. Usually, the gun barrel and the axe handle were combined. This shaft held the **trigger**.

The firing **mechanisms** varied, too. Some were flintlocks. These fired a shot by scraping a piece of flint against steel to create sparks.

Swords with guns attached to them were popular with European hunters in the 1700s. On these weapons, the gun's barrel ran partway along the sword's blade. Near the sword's handle were the trigger and the flintlock firing mechanism.

Some inventors even combined guns with furniture! A steel chest designed in the 1800s was created to keep

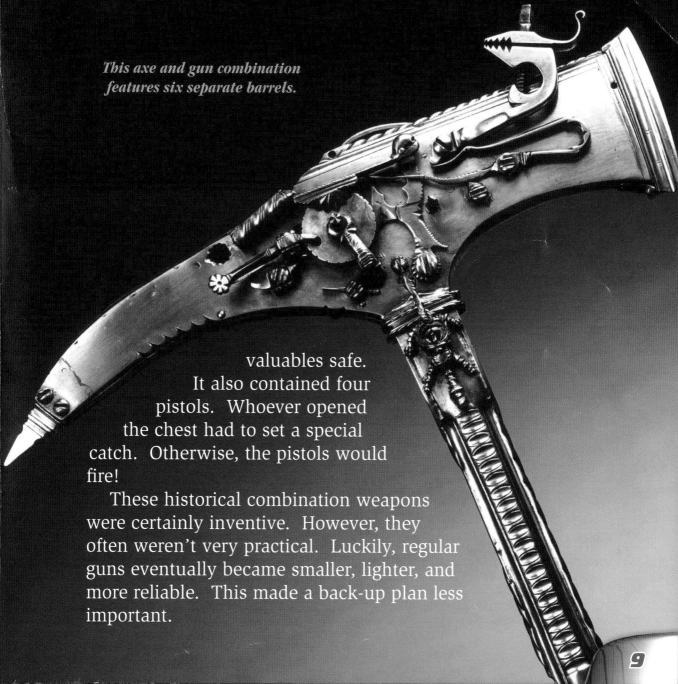

This axe and gun combination features six separate barrels.

valuables safe. It also contained four pistols. Whoever opened the chest had to set a special catch. Otherwise, the pistols would fire!

These historical combination weapons were certainly inventive. However, they often weren't very practical. Luckily, regular guns eventually became smaller, lighter, and more reliable. This made a back-up plan less important.

Artillery

An 81mm mortar

Modern special guns are much more high-tech than the old sword and pistol combination weapons. Have you ever heard of a mortar or a howitzer? These are artillery weapons.

Artillery is a big category of today's special weapons. These weapons have greater force and range than personal weapons. They are primarily used by the military. Artillery is classified as light, medium, or heavy depending on its size.

Modern artillery developed from cannons. An artillery weapon has a large **bore**. So, it can fire large **projectiles**. Sometimes the bore is smooth. Other times it is rifled, or grooved.

Artillery weapons are loaded with shells. A single shell is called a round. Shells are larger versions of the cartridges used in rifles and handguns.

CALIBER OR GAUGE?

Firearms and their ammunition can be organized by size. Caliber describes the distance across the bore of a rifle, handgun, or piece of artillery. The size of a shotgun bore is called gauge (GAYJ). These measurements are given in millimeters (mm) or in decimals of an inch.

Caliber and gauge also describe the size of the proper ammunition for each weapon. One popular handgun cartridge is 9mm. But an artillery shell can be more than 200mm!

A 120mm mortar round

The M198 howitzer fires two rounds per minute.

Handheld guns shoot **projectiles** fast and straight. But some artillery weapons fire shells in a big arc instead. So, the shells rise up into the air and then fall down onto their target. This allows them to hit targets behind obstacles. Different kinds of artillery fire shells at different speeds and distances.

The howitzer is a famous type of artillery weapon. It fires very large shells from a long barrel. Some howitzers can fire at targets up to 18 miles (29 km) away. That's more than 300 football fields!

Mortars are a smaller type of artillery. They can be light enough to carry by hand. They have smaller barrels than howitzers. And they fire in a much higher arc. So, the shells don't go as far.

Obviously, artillery weapons are much larger than regular guns. Often, they are too heavy to hold while firing. They can also be difficult to move. So, some are mounted on a set of wheels. Others are mounted on a base, rails, a land vehicle, or a ship.

Rockets and Grenades

Some types of artillery fire special kinds of ammunition. Rocket launchers are similar to mortars and howitzers. In those weapons, shells are **propelled** by explosions inside the barrel. That gives them all the power they need to reach their targets.

But rocket artillery fires self-propelled ammunition. The ammunition shoots out of the barrel with an initial explosion. But it still has more power to use, which gives it greater range.

Rocket artillery can be huge and mounted on trucks or other vehicles. These bigger systems can strike targets more than 180 miles (300 km) away.

*The AT-4 rocket launcher is an antitank weapon.
When fired, nothing should be within 16 feet (5 m)
of the back of the weapon!*

Bazookas required two users. One person loaded
the weapon and the other aimed and fired it.

Soldiers also use smaller, shoulder-mounted rocket launchers. These are more like traditional guns. The most famous is the bazooka.

Bazookas were used during **World War II** and the **Korean War**. They look like long metal pipes with handles. Like a pipe, both the back and front ends are open.

An ordinary gun creates **recoil** when it is fired. The force of the explosion pushes back on the user. Rockets create a lot of force. But the bazooka's open back end lets the force escape. This protects the user from recoil.

Other artillery weapons fire explosive grenades without using rockets. These weapons can be mounted on rifles or handheld like shotguns. Launchers send grenades farther and higher than soldiers can throw them.

Not all grenades are explosive. Some launchers fire grenades that just make smoke. During riots, police use launchers to shoot tear gas grenades. This helps stop disorder without harming anyone.

The MK19 grenade launcher can fire 40 grenades per minute.

Electroshock Weapons

Whenever possible, police want to stop criminals without injury or loss of life. So, they only use firearms as a last resort or for self-defense. Like tear gas grenades, electroshock weapons are **nonlethal** police weapons. Electroshock weapons such as Tasers offer a less dangerous option than firearms.

Tasers are about the size and shape of a pistol. But they don't **ignite** explosive powder, so they're not firearms. Instead, pulling the **trigger** releases gases that

Law enforcement and military personnel receive special training for electroshock weapons. Often, this includes experiencing the shock!

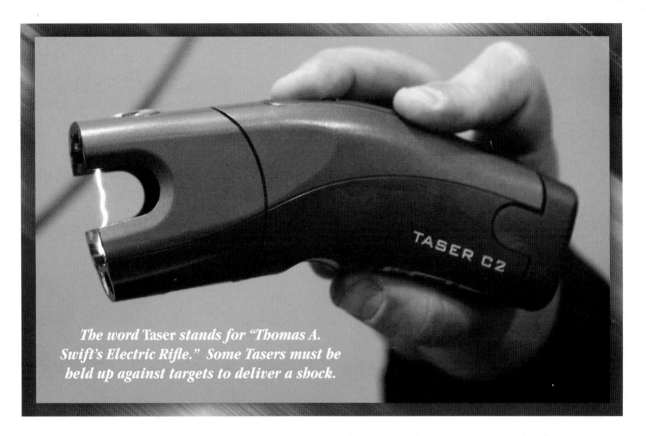

The word Taser *stands for "Thomas A. Swift's Electric Rifle." Some Tasers must be held up against targets to deliver a shock.*

propel small darts with barbs on them. These are like little claws that grab onto the target.

At the end of the darts are two electrodes. They stay attached to the gun by two long wires. The gun sends powerful bursts of electric current through the wires and into the target. This prevents the person's muscles from working properly. A criminal can't move for several seconds while being "tased." This helps police catch the person.

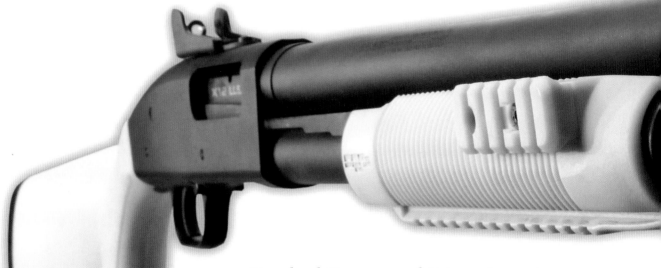

The Taser X12 is a 12-gauge shotgun. It fires eXtended Range Electronic Projectile cartridges. These shock the target for 20 seconds.

Standard Tasers can hit targets up to 35 feet (11 m) away. But police have weapons with longer ranges.

A new type of electroshock weapon is fired from a shotgun. It gives police and soldiers much more range. These guns fire **projectiles** that are similar to shotgun shells. They can reach targets up to 100 feet (30 m) away. And, the shells are not attached to the gun by wires.

There is some controversy over the use of electroshock weapons. Some critics say they are more painful than

supporters claim. Others argue they can be misused since they don't leave injury marks. The **United Nations** has criticized their use for torture. But, police say electroshock weapons save them from having to use deadlier force.

Guns Underwater

Soldiers and spies have relied on special weapons designed to fire underwater! Many were first created during the **Cold War**. At the time, the Soviet and American militaries were in an arms race. Each raced to develop better weapons. And each side was worried about an underwater attack.

Regular guns can fire underwater. But the bullets don't travel far. So in the 1960s and 1970s, Soviet and American designers worked to solve this problem.

The Americans developed the Underwater Defense Gun. It fired pointed darts. These had a range of about 30 feet (9 m) underwater.

The Russians invented the SPP-1, which fired darts called "flying nails." Each dart had a blunt end. This forced water away from the dart's sides when fired. With less water touching it, there was less drag to slow it down. So, the dart could travel 50 feet (15 m). A version of this gun is still used by Russian combat divers today.

Sound underwater was another problem designers faced. Shock waves from a gun's blast could damage a diver's hearing. The noise might also alert enemies to the diver's position. So, the underwater guns had sealed chambers. This feature muffled the explosion underwater and silenced the gun above water.

Today, the Navy SEALs use pistols such as the M11 Sig Sauer P-228. It is specially designed to resist the effects of water.

Tranquilizer Guns

Another gun that fires darts is a tranquilizer gun, or capture gun. Each dart carries a chemical **injection**. So, game wardens and other animal workers use tranquilizer guns to **sedate** wildlife.

These guns got their start in New Zealand. There in 1959, Colin Murdoch was studying wild goats. The young veterinarian wanted to take samples without capturing or harming the goats. And, he wanted to inject a safe sedative from far away. So, Murdoch worked to create a humane dart-and-gun system.

Murdoch invented a gun that fired a small **syringe** instead of a cartridge. It was also possible to adjust the force of the shot. That way, it didn't injure different sized animals. When the syringe hit an animal, it injected the chemicals. The animal would fall asleep until they wore off.

Park rangers, zookeepers, and others choose their sedatives carefully. They must use the right types and amounts of

chemicals. Too little might not affect an animal. Too much could harm it. This uncertainty is why tranquilizer guns are not used on people. A police officer could not count on it affecting everyone the same way or in the same amount of time.

Tranquilizer guns are used to capture dangerous animals, such as bears and wolves, that have entered public areas.

Flare Guns

Some guns are used for sending signals instead of hitting targets. One of these is the flare gun. Flare guns work like fireworks!

Explosives have been used as signals since the invention of gunpowder. But the modern flare gun wasn't invented until 1877. That year, US Navy officer Edward Very created a short-barreled pistol that could fire flares. These became known as Very pistols.

Modern flare guns still look like Very pistols. A flare is loaded in the **breech**. The **trigger** activates a small hammer, which strikes a detonating cap. This explosion shoots the flare and **ignites** it.

Flares can burn brightly for a long period of time. And like fireworks, they can burn in many different colors.

In the military, the colors can be used to send different messages. And sometimes, flares are used to light up a target. Outside the military, they're usually fired to signal for help.

Flare guns are not meant to be weapons. But they can be dangerous. Even when fired safely in the air, flares can start fires. So, only shoot a flare gun to signal a real emergency.

Flare guns are an important tool for attracting attention during an emergency.

Modern Combination Guns

A shotgun disguised as a cane

Like the old shield and pistol combination weapons, guns today come in some surprising forms. Have you ever seen a gun that looks like an umbrella? How about one that looks like a cane? These sound like tales from spy movies. But they're actually real!

Small guns that look like pens have been around since the 1920s. Umbrellas and canes have also been made into guns. The handle becomes the barrel, and the **projectile** must be small. Other guns have been combined with gloves, rings, flashlights, and even lipstick.

In the United States, the government regulates guns like these. A special category covers pen guns, knife guns, umbrella guns, and more. To own one, a person must pay a tax and pass a background check. These rules come from the National Firearms Act (NFA).

The NFA also applies to artillery such as mortars and howitzers. And it covers certain military guns. This includes the powerful AK-47 assault rifle. The NFA helps the government track these weapons.

For many gun collectors, the extra steps are worth it. Special weapons can be fascinating to study and admire!

SPY STORY

In 1978, a Bulgarian writer named Georgi Markov died mysteriously. In his body was found a small poison pellet. Authorities think Markov was shot using an umbrella gun. This was a spy story come to life!

GLOSSARY

bore - the long, hollow inside of a gun barrel.

breech - the part of a firearm at the back of the barrel.

Cold War - a period of tension and hostility between the United States and its allies and the Soviet Union and its allies after World War II.

ignite - to set on fire.

inject - to force a fluid into the body, usually with a needle or something sharp. An injection is something that is injected.

Korean War - a war fought in North and South Korea from 1950 to 1953. The US government sent troops to help South Korea.

mechanism - a system of parts working together.

nonlethal - of or relating to not causing death.

projectile - an object that can be thrown or shot out.

propel - to drive forward or onward by some force.

recoil - the sharp, violent reaction or springing back of a gun when fired.

sedate - to cause to become quiet or calm.

syringe (suh-RIHNJ) - a tube used to put fluids into a body or take them out.

trigger - the small lever pulled back by the finger to fire a gun.

United Nations - a group of nations formed in 1945. Its goals are peace, human rights, security, and social and economic development.

World War II - from 1939 to 1945, fought in Europe, Asia, and Africa. Great Britain, France, the United States, the Soviet Union, and their allies were on one side. Germany, Italy, Japan, and their allies were on the other side.

To learn more about guns and special weapons, visit ABDO Publishing Company online. Web sites about guns and special weapons are featured on our Book Links page. These links are routinely monitored and updated to provide the most current information available.
www.abdopublishing.com

INDEX